THE INNER WORK OF WORK

COACHING YOURSELF FOR IMPROVED PERFORMANCE

Being Your Best

Michael Baroff

BK

Berrett-Koehler Communications, Inc.

Berrett-Koehler Communications, Inc.
450 Sansome Street, Suite 1200
San Francisco, CA 94111
Phone: 415-288-0260
Fax: 415-362-2512

ORDERING INFORMATION

Please send orders to Berrett-Koehler Communications, P.O. Box 565, Williston, VT 05495. Or place your order by calling 800-929-2929, faxing 802-864-7626, or visiting www.bkconnection.com.

Special discounts are available on quantity purchases.
For details, call 800-929-2929.

Printed in the United States of America on acid-free recycled paper.

ISBN 1-58376-153-5

CONTENTS

Welcome to the Inner Work of Work

You have in your hands a guidebook for dealing with some of the most common issues you will face in the workplace. As you explore these issues you will embark on a journey that will expand and deepen your relationship to the realities of work and, most assuredly, give you an advantage in a changing and competitive job market.

In this guidebook, I present prevailing human resource development, training, and organizational development ideas in a simple and direct manner. The intent is to give you access to and an enhanced personal understanding of the factors executives and managers encounter in trying to improve a company's performance through the efforts of the people like you who work in that company.

The material is written in a format that will enable you to think about, reflect on, and come up with your own perspectives and solutions. This approach is the essence of "inner work."

Though it appears to be simple and direct, doing inner work will require your focus and attention if you are to stretch beyond your current capabilities. With this understanding, I trust you will come to appreciate the value of not only reading but also working through the material. As you use this guidebook, appreciate that you will gain confidence both through the process of developing your own insights and from the specific results you achieve by acting on those insights.

Let's look for a moment at the connection between inner work and improved performance. While on the job, your focus and attention are, by and large, on creating tangible bottom-line results, products, services, revenue, and profit. You strive to produce something of value or get things done in a timely and cost-effective manner. You attend meetings, plan, organize, and perform tasks and activities to achieve results. Of course, all this is what work is externally about, but what is behind or underneath all this activity?

The focus on inner work puts the responsibility on you to reflect on, then stretch beyond your usual approach and come up with responses to essential work issues such as the following: What motivates me to succeed? What do I need to learn in order to develop and grow? Where I am going in my career? How can I communicate more effectively, so that I am understood? How do I deal with conflicts? Where do I fit into the big picture? How can I take a leadership role? What is the meaning or purpose in what I do? Whom am I serving by the work I do? Am I manifesting my creativity? Am I experiencing joy in what I do?

Some of these questions may seem a bit philosophical for typical work-related conversation, but they are the essence of what inner work is about. Inner work is about becoming aware of the qualities, capabilities, and attributes you bring to what you do and creating a sense of personal meaning and commitment from that awareness.

Ask yourself where you are on the following continuum in your relationship to your work:

1. Are you just showing up in order to survive?
2. Are you interested and engaged in what you do?
3. Are you willing and able to push beyond your limits and boundaries?
4. Are you fully committed to achieving and succeeding with purpose, meaning, and a clear sense of inner direction and personal satisfaction?

By doing inner work you can shift your perceptions and working relationships to improve your performance by coming to terms with what serves or doesn't serve you, those you work with, and the company you work for, and then deciding what to do about it.

You may ask yourself why it is so important to take time to think about and reflect on workplace issues. Consider what has been going on in workplaces over the past few years. There is widespread and deep change in expectations about work and the social contract between employers and employees. To compete in the global marketplace, employers are restructuring their businesses, reorganizing departments and functions, reengineering work processes, and redeploying people. There is also an emerging perspective that employees are no longer simply "human resources," but rather are "human capital," whose value is a function of the productivity they create for the organization that employs them. These dynamics are neither good nor bad; they are just the way it currently is. Although any guarantee of lifelong employment in any one company is nearly gone in all industries, including the government sector, there is also an emerging expectation on the part of employers that employees be accountable for their performance and that employees be stakeholders in the results they produce. Employers are looking to recruit and retain the best employees, who are able to take responsibility for their own job development and performance improvement.

From an employee's point of view, another set of expectations is emerging about quality of personal, professional, and spiritual life. You spend a large portion of your daily life in the pursuit of and the doing of work, and the workplace can provide you with much of the grist for not only job and career development but also personal development. As the nature of work has evolved from purely industrial to "knowledge-based" your individual and our collective effectiveness and productivity have come to depend less on the sweat of our physical labor than on the essence of our being. Thus, it is also your spirit that may now desire to be nurtured.

This guidebook, *Being Your Best*, addresses the *attitudes* of personal success that are determined by self-awareness and the choices you make. This guidebook enables you to come to terms with who you are, what you have to offer, and where you want to go in your work life. You will explore your beliefs about work, what motivates you to succeed, how to use your creativity and intuition, tap into your energy and feelings, clarify the roles you play at work, learn how to adapt to change, and create the outcomes and lifestyle you want.

You may find value in the other guidebooks in this series:

Getting Along with Others addresses the *behavior and skills* that enhance communication and relationships with other people. You will examine how your behavior is perceived by others, learn how to develop trust, enhance how you listen and develop rapport when communicating, set the stage for dealing with differences and conflict, and present yourself assertively when working with others.

Contributing to Your Company's Success addresses the *organizational dynamics* that create and support a productive work environment. This guidebook gives you the tools to determine where you fit into a company's big picture. You will learn how to work as part of a team, understand how a company evaluates the bottom line, determine how to add value in what you do, and develop your own approach to being a leader.

As you read through each guidebook and explore the issues connected to your work-related personal, professional, and spiritual growth, I invite you to consider the following overarching question:

How can I approach my work life as an ongoing quest to maintain awareness of my inner mental, emotional, and essential processes while coming to terms with what in my experience nurtures me and what I must move through or beyond in order to change or improve my on-the-job performance?

The guidebooks provide you with a road map to refer to as you embark on this journey of performance improvement. You are the one in the driver's seat, choosing the milestones you want to reach, how slow or fast to go, and when and where to make a turn or take a rest.

What Does It Mean to Coach Yourself?

When you think about the role of a coach, you are likely to imagine someone who works with a sports team or an individual athlete. Some people who work out at a local gym use a personal trainer or coach to help keep them on a schedule and a regimen for cardiovascular, aerobic, and weight training in order to trim down, tone up, and develop strength. The goal of coaching is to improve performance. Interestingly, people who use coaches tend to be those who are already motivated and committed to improving and thus attaining the highest performance possible for themselves.

In the workplace, it is typically executives who engage the services of a coach. One would think that executives would already have achieved success and high performance. However, as with the athletes and teams who use a coach, it is those on the path of development who are aware of their own limits, yet know they could do better if given a little assistance from someone who has their interests and goals in mind.

Viewed from a larger perspective, coaching focuses on helping you achieve three overall goals:

- To become responsible for your own ongoing development
- To achieve and maintain productive interpersonal relationships
- To commit to achieving organizational goals through improved performance

To achieve these goals, it is important for you to clarify and appreciate the value you offer through the work you do, develop ongoing and supportive ways of communicating with your co-workers, and continually focus on how your performance affects organizational goals.

Let's explore the dynamics of a coaching relationship. The qualities of a coach include being trustworthy, open and honest, sincere, committed, and nonjudgmental. A coach asks questions, challenges, listens, pays attention, and stays focused on the acknowledged purpose. It is important for you to incorporate the qualities of a coach into your own mindset. By learning to coach yourself, you will be able to make changes or improvements in your attitude about your work, your behavior at work, your ongoing job, your career or professional development, your performance and achievements, and your personal sense of success.

Ultimately, the effort you must make comes down to doing an "inside out" job. That is, you—not your manager, supervisor, teacher, trainer, or coach—have to make the change or improvement. Likewise, who else but you could know, determine, or care most about your path of growth and the pace at which you move along that path?

Who but you has the most capacity to listen to what you think and feel? I firmly believe that the answers to your work-related questions and challenges are within you.

What might it mean for you to learn how to coach yourself? At first the idea may seem like a contradiction or an oxymoron. I don't mean to suggest that this process should be done entirely alone or in isolation from what is going on where you work. Rather, I believe it is important to create a climate and expectations for integrating your inner work into your day-to-day work-performance improvement efforts.

With this belief in mind, I have developed what I call "Coaching Points." These Coaching Points are analogous to the coaching points someone playing a sport or doing a personal fitness program would work on to improve performance. For instance, a tennis player might practice specific components of the game such as the serve, forehand, backhand, and mental focus in order to improve overall performance. Someone on a health and fitness program might work on diet, endurance, muscle strength, and flexibility in order to enhance well-being. In either situation, the coaching process involves structured practice on a series of integrated exercises to achieve an overall goal.

This guidebook is designed to walk you through a series of "Coaching Points" that will help you gain deeper insight and ability to directly address your on-the-job situations. In the process, you will learn how to coach yourself for improved performance.

Why Be Your Best?

B*eing Your Best* helps you examine your attitudes, beliefs, and values, consider what you know or need to learn, expand your limits and boundaries, and solidify your sense of self and motivation—so that you can be your best in the work you do.

Many career counselors will readily admit that no single test or assessment can really tell you what you are good at or the job you should be doing. By working through the material in this guidebook, you will be able to assess for yourself what is meaningful to you and then take action appropriately. *Being Your Best* supports you in being your own career coach.

Are you beginning a new job, newly entering the workforce, or looking to make a job change? Use this guidebook as part of your own employee-orientation program. Examine how your current beliefs, energy, feelings, motivation, needs, and wants are affecting your on-the-job performance and ability to adapt to change.

Are you due for a performance appraisal? Your company may have a standardized performance appraisal process that allows you to discuss with your supervisor or manager how you are evaluated on various performance criteria. Regardless of the format of your appraisal, by working through this guidebook, you can identify areas where you need to improve, then set clear guidelines and time frames for your own development. By doing so, you will demonstrate to your supervisor a willingness to take responsibility for your own performance, and you will be better prepared to discuss developmental opportunities.

Perhaps your supervisor has evaluated some of your work as "below expectations" or only "meeting expectations" and indicates that she feels that you don't seem motivated to do better or that your attitude seems to get in the way of your performance. You may be frustrated because you don't know exactly what she means or because there are things going on in your life that you don't feel comfortable talking about with her. By taking yourself through the Coaching Points in this guidebook you will explore, for instance, how your assumptions and beliefs affect your behavior, what influences you to succeed, and how to maintain your energy and sense of humor. As you take the initiative to understand more about yourself, you will be able to identify what stands in your way, find it easier to discuss your appraisal with your supervisor, and make changes to improve your performance.

Why is focusing on your career important? Different from a generation or two ago, it is not uncommon for people currently in the labor force to have many careers over their work life, meaning different types of work, not just different jobs within the same field. In fact, there is even an expectation that the generation of people in the workforce now will not retire as they reach senior-citizen status, but rather will begin new careers or expand on avocations they have developed during their adult life.

To be your best is to consider yourself an asset or valuable commodity that can develop and produce a greater return on investment. Your most important resource is your talent, and what you earn will depend on what you learn.

An all-too-common dynamic occurs within the ranks of employees in organizations undergoing change. A majority of people typically take a wait-and-see approach to the impending change, often with the attitude that "the more things change, the more they stay the same." A small group of people deal with the situation by holding tight, resisting, fearing, or rebelling against the change, often spreading rumors and gossiping. Still another small number of people seek to keep informed about what's going on, assess their options, and take a proactive approach so that they become part of the change. When the change and transition occur, guess which group (a) gets the better jobs, (b) is likely to be out of a job, or (c) gets what's left over whether they like it or not? *Being Your Best* helps move you along the path so that you will be part of the "A" group. The best way to cope with change is to anticipate it.

Regardless of what work you do or how long you have been doing it, keeping your long-range career path in mind is important not only to you, but also to your employer. It is common knowledge that during times of impending organizational change, it is the most competent and marketable employee who is at the forefront of looking out for her or his options. Recognize that it is in the best interest of employers to keep the most competent and conscientious employees engaged in thinking about how they can support any organizational change and be ready to deal with it on their own.

Getting Started

This guidebook is comprised of a series of what I call "Coaching Points," each focusing on an area that influences how people commonly approach work. You will find a Coaching Point on, for example, behavior, another on trust, and so on. There are 20 Coaching Points in all and each one takes you step by step through a process of thinking about and reflecting on an area that has direct impact on your work. Each Coaching Point concludes by asking you to develop an action plan based on what you have learned during the process.

Below I give a brief introduction to the Coaching Point concept and its various parts, explaining how a Coaching Point is designed and giving you some ideas about how to work through them.

First, notice that each Coaching Point is formatted to contain the following elements:

- A *Definition* defines or describes a main idea or concept.
- A *Simple Truth* expresses the essential meaning underlying the Coaching Point.
- *For Your Consideration* presents a probing question, thought, or example that reinforces the practical implications of the Coaching Point.
- A sequence of *First Steps* offers ways you can begin to explore the Coaching Point. Some steps suggest things to think about now or things to do when certain situations arise.
- A *Reflection* prompts you to rely on your own inner guidance in thinking more deeply about the Coaching Point and applying it.
- The *Next Step* encourages you to take immediate action to follow up and implement the Coaching Point.

The sequence in which each of these elements is presented is designed to allow you to explore, unfold, integrate, and apply the learning associated with each Coaching Point. The process will support you in coming up with your own insights and actions.

It will be helpful to have a writing pad, notebook, or journal at hand in which to write down your thoughts, responses, and insights as you go through the material.

Before you begin, select a comfortable and quiet place to read and work through the material. Allow yourself a minimum of 15 minutes to work through each Coaching Point.

If you don't have the time or don't feel the need to go through the material in a structured manner, you can rely on the guidebook as a desk reference or on-the-job performance aid. Keep the guidebook visible on your bookcase as a handy resource to reinforce essential expectations about your on-the-job performance. You can always pick up the guidebook, begin anywhere, follow your inclinations, and trust that you will learn what you need when you need it.

To help you get the most out of doing the inner work presented in this book, I walk you through a sample Coaching Point. In this walk through (which follows) I do two things. First, I offer some suggestions for how to approach each element of the Coaching Point. I refer to these suggestions as "Coaching Prompts." Second, I share some brief excerpts of my own thoughts and reflections that are taken from my personal self-coaching work. I label these responses "Thoughts." My purpose here is to model what inner work *can* look like, not what it *should* look like. I encourage you to find your own, unique approach to doing inner work.

Before you embark on your own inner work, let me leave you with this thought. Doing inner work is not always easy, but neither is it complicated. It simply involves taking the time to step back from the automatic, quick and often hurried reactions you may have to issues and situations before you take action. Inner work allows you to take on the role of observer in order to become more aware of both your thoughts and how they are translated into action. In cultivating your ability to act as a reflective observer of your own thinking you become your own coach—a coach who is honest, sincere, committed, and nonjudgmental, who listens and asks probing questions, and who can be trusted to keep your best interests and purposes in mind.

Congratulations! You are about to begin a journey of self-awareness and development that will serve you throughout your work life.

▪ *Coaching Point Walk Through* ▪

BELIEFS are strongly held perceptions, attitudes, and opinions.

SIMPLE TRUTH

What you believe affects how you behave.

Coaching Prompt ➤ As you read the statements, consider what stands out for you in the wording of the description or definition. Does the Simple Truth ring true for you? If so, recall a situation in your personal experience that makes it real for you. If not, what situation in your personal experience suggests a different way to interpret the statement?

Thoughts ✍ Interesting. Are beliefs only opinions? Can I change a belief? Aren't some of my beliefs fundamental to who I am?

I believe that doing good work should get rewarded. I guess I expect this of myself and the people I work with. I have resented it when I don't get what I feel is due me, especially when I see others get recognized for what seems like doing less. Has this resentment shown up in my work?

➡ FOR YOUR CONSIDERATION

Beliefs about work may include the following: work hard to get ahead; do what you love and money will follow; accept opportunities as they come along; play by the rules; question authority; it's not right unless it's perfect; get by with good enough; work builds character; it's only a job; it's who you know, not what you know; everyone has unique talents to offer.

Coaching Prompt ➤ Think about the practical implications and consequences of the For Your Consideration statement. Again, recall a personal experience that either reinforces the message of the statement for you or suggests a different perspective. Remember, the statements are only guides; it is your experience that is real for you.

Thoughts ✍ I really didn't put my full effort into that last project. Figured I'd just get through it and get it over with. I didn't expect to get much recognition either way, but still, I'm not satisfied. Maybe I don't really believe that getting by with good enough is OK, but on that last project I guess I acted as if I did.

By thinking more about that last project, I realize that I expect a lot from myself and others and that I get frustrated when things just don't come together or I don't really know why I'm having to work so hard without getting some acknowledgment. Sometimes that makes it difficult to accept what my work group produces. I wonder what it would take to really feel satisfied?

FIRST STEPS

1. What are your beliefs about work?
2. Who has influenced these beliefs?
3. What circumstances or experiences have influenced these beliefs?
4. Have your beliefs stayed the same or changed over time?
5. Do any of these beliefs conflict with or contradict each other?

Coaching Prompt ➤ Read through each of the First Steps and make some notes to yourself in response to the questions or suggestions. Perhaps there are specific resources or information in your workplace that can help you move through each step.

Thoughts ✍ Both my parents expected a lot from me and were critical when I didn't meet their expectations. They had very different attitudes about work, though. My dad thought that life was a struggle and that you had to make things happen or they wouldn't get done. My mom took things as they came along and was more accepting of how things went. I wasn't sure what to do to be appreciated.

I guess I sometimes can't figure out whether I should work hard or just let it be. I end up being somewhat frustrated either way.

REFLECTION

How do your beliefs affect your ability to be your best at work? Could it be that some of these beliefs no longer serve you in your work life?

Coaching Prompt ➤ Before you explore the Reflection, take a deep breath and get into a relaxed and open state of mind. Then read the statement and take a few minutes to look within yourself to explore any meaning or significance the statement has for you.

Thoughts ✍ Maybe I can figure out a way to balance both perspectives. Sometimes it may be more productive to push hard and other times it may be best to let things be as they are for a while. Might minimize my frustration!

NEXT STEP

List questions to ask yourself about any old or conflicting beliefs that no longer serve you or impede your ability to be your best. How might you change your perception in order move beyond or through these impediments?

Coaching Prompt ➤ You should now be ready to outline some Next Step actions. Be very specific when you write down each action. Make an agreement with yourself as to when, where, and with whom to follow up with actions. Appreciate and acknowledge your progress no matter what pace you move at on your journey.

Thoughts ✍ What are the signs I'm getting frustrated? Do I always have to have things go my way? It makes sense to get everyone else's take on how things are going. There may be something I'm not aware of that might affect how to proceed. I will try to be aware of what it is that is causing me to be frustrated and not let it get to me or hold me back from participating in the meetings. I'll express what's going on with me to the others and ask to discuss how to proceed within that context. As a group we can decide which things to push on and which things to allow to take their course.

COACHING SESSION ONE

■

Enabling Yourself to Succeed

In this session you will explore the following Coaching Points:

- BELIEFS
- NEEDS AND WANTS
- POWER AND PRIVILEGE
- GROWTH
- MOTIVATION

Each of us comes to the workplace with a unique set of experiences and expectations that affect who we are and what we do. This session helps you explore some of the fundamental issues that will affect your ability to succeed on the job.

Your performance is influenced by many factors, including the beliefs you hold, the needs and wants you have, the goals and desires you seek, as well as your sense of personal power. The challenge is to become aware of how your own perceptions either help or hinder your personal, professional, and spiritual growth.

Your ability to tap into these powerful underlying forces will help you come to terms with what is motivating you to succeed and supporting your ability to be your best.

BELIEFS are strongly held *perceptions*, *attitudes*, and *opinions*.

> SIMPLE TRUTH
>
> *What you believe affects how you behave.*

FOR YOUR CONSIDERATION

Beliefs about work may include the following: work hard to get ahead; do what you love and money will follow; accept opportunities as they come along; play by the rules; question authority; it's not right unless it's perfect; get by with good enough; work builds character; it's only a job; it's who you know, not what you know; everyone has unique talents to offer.

FIRST STEPS

1. What are your beliefs about work?
2. Who has influenced these beliefs?
3. What circumstances or experiences have influenced these beliefs?
4. Have your beliefs stayed the same or changed over time?
5. Do any of these beliefs conflict with or contradict each other?

REFLECTION

How do your beliefs affect your ability to be your best at work? Could it be that some of these beliefs no longer serve you in your work life?

NEXT STEP

List questions to ask yourself about any old or conflicting beliefs that no longer serve you or impede your ability to be your best. How might you change your perception in order move beyond or through these impediments?

NEEDS are the *desires* that you strive to fulfill.

WANTS are *goals* that you can back up with action.

SIMPLE TRUTH

Allow your needs to influence your wants, rather than have your wants influence your needs.

FOR YOUR CONSIDERATION

Needing to continually improve your skills in a changing work environment is different than *wanting* a particular job, position, or title for the status it offers.

FIRST STEPS

Assess your ability to meet basic *needs*:

1. To what extent are you able to take care of your basic needs for *survival* and *security*?
2. How have you developed and nurtured *working relationships*?
3. What are you doing to *achieve* your personal potential?

Assess your *wants*:

1. Is what you want *possible* to achieve?
2. Is what you want worth the time and *energy* to pursue?
3. How will getting what you want fulfill your ultimate desire?

REFLECTION

Take a mental inventory of all the resources (people, circumstances, and situations) that support your ability to be your best.

NEXT STEP

Describe what you can do to develop or enhance the support you need or want.

POWER is the ability to *influence* people, situations, and outcomes.

PRIVILEGE is the *advantage* you may have as a consequence of your power.

SIMPLE TRUTH

The abuse of power and privilege is at the root of most human conflict.

FOR YOUR CONSIDERATION

Power exists in many forms: • Emotional • Financial • Healing • Imagination • Information • Knowledge • Language • Social • Spiritual • Will

Privilege may be connected to your gender, race, social and economic status, or group affiliation.

FIRST STEPS

1. What are your sources of power at work, and how do you use them?
2. What are the sources of your privilege at work, and how do you use them?
3. Which types of power are you uncomfortable with?
4. Which sources of power do you need to develop?

REFLECTION

Recall a work situation when you gave up your power to another. Recall a situation when you exerted your power over another.

NEXT STEP

Describe how you can use your power and privilege for a greater good in the work you do.

GROWTH is a combination of *learning* new attitudes, behaviors, and skills and appreciating yourself as you are.

> **SIMPLE TRUTH**
>
> *On your path of growth, expect to take steps backward as well as forward.*

FOR YOUR CONSIDERATION

Have you followed a predetermined plan of education and job goals? Have you taken opportunities as they were offered to you? Have you experienced a balance of each approach to your growth?

FIRST STEPS

Consider how you have grown to be the person you are today:

1. What life experiences have helped you understand who you are?
2. What milestones mark the turning points in your life that brought you:
   - To the type of work you are doing?
   - To the company you work at?
   - To the specific job you are now doing?
3. What lessons have you had to relearn? Have you had to relearn them once, twice, or many times?

REFLECTION

Who have you been? Who do you think you are now? Who do others think you are? Who do you want to become?

NEXT STEP

List questions to ask yourself or things you need to do to continue on or change your current path of growth.

MOTIVATION is what influences and supports your *performance* on the job.

People are typically motivated by a combination of the following factors:

- Recognition and appreciation
- Achievement
- Money and compensation
- The nature of the work itself
- Being given responsibility
- Security and stability
- Personal goals
- Beliefs about success or failure
- Job satisfaction

SIMPLE TRUTH

All motivation ultimately comes from within yourself.

FOR YOUR CONSIDERATION

Take the time to celebrate and reward your own performance on a regular basis.

FIRST STEPS

To tap into what motivates you on the job:

1. Prioritize each of the factors listed above as to the degree to which it motivates your work performance: "most," "somewhat," or least."
2. Assess if there is anything about your work policies, procedures, or practices that contributes to any lack of motivation you may have on the job.
3. Consider how to address what stands in the way of your feeling motivated.

REFLECTION

Complete the sentence: "I last did my best when . . . ."

NEXT STEP

Describe ways you can motivate and reward yourself on the job.

SESSION SYNTHESIS

- What insights or new awareness did you gain in this session?
- What key learnings are associated with those insights?
- Which Coaching Points or aspects were easier to work through?
- Which Coaching Points or aspects were more difficult to work through?
- What specific steps or actions have you already taken? What occurred or didn't occur?
- What specific steps or actions do you feel most resistant to taking? What is underlying that resistance?
- What questions or concerns remain unanswered for you right now? What are you going to do about it?

COACHING SESSION TWO

■

Learning How to Improve

In this session you will explore the following Coaching Points:

- KNOW-HOW
- CREATIVITY
- INTUITION
- JUDGMENT
- ATTENTION

The next component in *Being Your Best* is about developing the capacity to "learn how to learn." Nowadays, becoming a lifelong learner is essential in order to keep up with the increasing expectations to perform work in a more timely, effective, and efficient manner.

The basis for learning how to improve your performance is to first explore what you know that enables you to do your current job and what you need to know in order to do what you want to do in the future. From there, three additional critical ingredients will contribute to your ability to improve your individual performance: using your creativity, trusting your intuition, and relying on your own judgment. These ingredients form the basis for demonstrating the confidence you have in yourself.

Finally, it is important, on a daily basis, to exercise your inner ability to focus on what is important and to design your outer environment to enhance your comfort and minimize unwanted distractions. By focusing your attention mentally and physically, you increase your potential for a higher level of performance. By not paying attention, you are apt to waste valuable time, energy, and resources on unproductive activities.

KNOW-HOW is being able to competently and confidently apply *knowledge* and demonstrate *skill* in the work you do.

SIMPLE TRUTH

The more you know, the more you realize how much you don't know.

FOR YOUR CONSIDERATION

The best way to learn something new is to have an immediate opportunity to use and practice that skill or knowledge.

FIRST STEPS

In acquiring any new knowledge or skill, appreciate that you will move through the following stages:

1. You must be *willing* and able to learn while being open to what you don't know.
2. You will need to go through a process to develop your knowledge and skills in a planned and thoughtful manner.
3. You will then *integrate* that knowledge and skill in *everyday practice* and be able to refine your performance with ongoing learning.

REFLECTION

Think of a work-related skill you have learned. Was the process of learning that skill difficult or easy? In what way and why? How did you know you really knew how to apply the skill?

NEXT STEP

Draft a statement describing what you do, what interests you, and/or what you want or need to learn in order to become more competent in the work you do or want to do.

CREATIVITY is the ability everyone has to *think about, organize,* and *express* ideas and actions in new ways.

SIMPLE TRUTH

Doing the same thing in the same way will get you consistency, not innovation.

FOR YOUR CONSIDERATION

Creativity can be applied to overcoming challenges, solving problems, and developing new options and opportunities in response to the limitations and frustration reflected by an attitude of "we don't do it like that here."

FIRST STEPS

When confronting a challenging situation or problem at work:

1. Ask questions to discover different approaches:
   - What if?
   - What else?
   - Why not?
2. Break old habits by:
   - Doing something new and different
   - Going somewhere you've never been
   - Talking with someone you don't know well
   - Trying to see what's around you as if for the first time
3. Hold off on forming an opinion or being critical of a new idea.
4. Take the risk of possibly being wrong and having to admit it.
5. Make imaginative connections between people, places, and things.

REFLECTION

What is the usual way you approach solving a work problem? Are there particular steps you take or techniques you use? What is preventing you from trying something new?

NEXT STEP

Describe some new ways you can creatively approach a current work-related challenge.

INTUITION is that subtle sense of *knowing* that allows you to make associations and connections without relying on rational analysis.

> **SIMPLE TRUTH**
>
> *Our ordinary senses are limited in perception, but our quiet mind expands without limit.*

FOR YOUR CONSIDERATION

Have you ever had a great idea while driving, showering, or walking leisurely? An intuitive solution or hunch often comes to us when we are doing something totally unconnected to the problem we are working on.

FIRST STEPS

When dealing with a challenging situation at work:

1. Sit quietly and listen to your thoughts, letting them flow freely across your mind.
2. Notice how your body is responding to each thought. Do you feel tight, relaxed, nervous, excited?
3. Assess the meaning and significance of your thoughts in relation to your bodily sensations.
4. "Test the reality" of your perceptions against what you logically think ought to happen or should be the right thing to do.
5. Recognize that what seems right and true to you now may change later on.

REFLECTION

Recall a work-related situation in which you followed a hunch. Then recall a situation in which you resisted your hunch. What happened or didn't happen as a result in either situation?

NEXT STEP

Consider a workplace problem or challenge that you have been trying to solve. Now sit quietly for five minutes and focus on your inhalation and exhalation of breath. After the five minutes, describe what is going through your mind.

JUDGMENT is your ability to *discern* and *evaluate* the significance of a particular incident or situation for yourself.

> **SIMPLE TRUTH**
>
> *We often judge ourselves by our intentions, others by our expectations.*

FOR YOUR CONSIDERATION

Though it is often helpful to ask for advice from others, appreciate that their advice is based on their experience, not yours.

FIRST STEPS

When dealing with a challenging situation at work:

1. Consider how your past experiences have helped to create the present work situation, but do not limit or define yourself by those experiences.
2. Reserve the right to make a value judgment as to whether something is right or wrong for you by considering the alternatives.
3. Be open to changing your mind on the basis of contrary evidence, feedback, or persuasive argument from others.
4. Appreciate that using your judgment is different from being judgmental or unduly critical of others.
5. Focus on what you can do in the here and now.

REFLECTION

What is most important to you about how you do your job? How might others interpret your priorities? How do you interpret others' behavior on the basis of your own priorities? Note whether you are using your judgment or being judgmental.

NEXT STEP

Think about a situation you are involved in or a decision you must make that might be considered either right or wrong. Describe the alternatives, and then make a judgment as to how to proceed.

ATTENTION is that state of mind that contributes to your ability to experience *peak performance* during your work day.

SIMPLE TRUTH

The challenge really is to work smarter, not harder.

FOR YOUR CONSIDERATION

Consider your relationship to time and space at work. How often does the phrase "I don't have enough time" reflect an inner conflict or lack of clarity about your needs, wants, or desired outcomes?

FIRST STEPS

To improve your attention at work:

1. Enhance your workspace with a good light source and a chair adjusted for your body; maintain a comfortably cool room temperature; and arrange your work with minimal clutter and disarray.
2. Plan your daily work: (a) categorize the outcomes you need to achieve as "short term," "mid term," or "long term"; (b) list the activities needed to achieve each outcome; (c) prioritize those activities in terms of how they contribute to achieving each particular outcome as "essential," "important," or "optional"; (d) act according to your daily priorities.
3. Write out and post positive messages, such as the following:
    - "I expect success."
    - "I trust my skills, knowledge and talent."
    - "Every problem is an opportunity for learning and growth."
    - "I am focused on my desired outcome."
4. Eat healthy, high-energy foods and stretch your body throughout the day.
5. Make time during the day to relax your mind and let it become receptive.

REFLECTION

Recall a time when you thought that you worked very hard, but nothing much resulted. Then think of a time when things seemed to happen by themselves, with hardly any effort on your part. Recall a time when you were totally absorbed in what you were doing. What were the circumstances surrounding these experiences? What were the factors that contributed to the different outcomes?

NEXT STEP

Make any changes in your work environment necessary to enhance your effectiveness. List your current work priorities and describe the factors that make achieving each outcome either easy or difficult to accomplish.

SESSION SYNTHESIS

- What insights or new awareness did you gain in this session?
- What key learnings are associated with those insights?
- Which Coaching Points or aspects were easier to work through?
- Which Coaching Points or aspects were more difficult to work through?
- What specific steps or actions have you already taken? What occurred or didn't occur?
- What specific steps or actions do you feel most resistant to taking? What is underlying that resistance?
- What questions or concerns remain unanswered for you right now? What are you going to do about it?

COACHING SESSION THREE

■

Coping With Challenges

In this session you will explore the following Coaching Points:

- ENERGY
- FEELINGS
- HUMOR
- SENSITIVITY
- YOU

A very important aspect of *Being Your Best* is successfully confronting and coping with everyday workplace challenges. Having a personal approach for dealing with difficult situations is essential. Each of us develops mechanisms at an early age for dealing with stress. Some ways can be helpful and nurturing; other ways may be less supportive or healthy. Being able to cope with stress and challenge enables you to maintain the grounding necessary for dealing with work-related situational demands, pressure, and change.

The basic ingredients for coping with challenge involve being aware of your energy level and feelings at all times, approaching situations with an appropriate sense of humor, understanding how unconscious or hidden aspects of your personality may affect your behavior, and then appreciating that, when all is said and done, you are the person who is ultimately responsible for your own performance and success.

ENERGY is the influence you project at any moment that either *connects* you with or *disconnects* you from other people.

SIMPLE TRUTH

What goes around comes around.

FOR YOUR CONSIDERATION

Companies try to isolate employees with negative attitudes because they tend to affect other people's performance and productivity.

FIRST STEPS

To assess your energy in the moment:

1. Sit quietly for a moment, take a deep breath, and close your eyes.
2. Notice what you are thinking, feeling, and experiencing at this moment. Are those thoughts and feelings:
   - Flowing smoothly one to another?
   - Pushing against each other?
   - Moving in all directions at once?
   - Harmonizing and in unity?
   - Silent and still?
3. Recognize that the energy projected by those thoughts and feelings will influence how other people relate with you in this moment.
4. Repeat these steps throughout the day.

REFLECTION

Recall the circumstances when you last felt that "all was right" at work. What was the energy you projected? What were the responses you received from others?

NEXT STEP

Describe what you can do to tap into your positive energy daily.

FEELINGS are the array of *sensations* or *emotions* that communicate *needs* and *wants* to your mind that then affect your *behavior.*

Negative feelings tend to express an intention to *exclude* something or someone and are often based on a fear of the unknown. Examples of negative feelings are apathy, hatred, shame, blame, regret, resentment, anger, and hostility.

Positive feelings tend to express an intention to *include.* Positive emotions are based on a desire for enjoyment and unity. Examples of positive feelings are interest, enthusiasm, empathy, action, and curiosity.

> SIMPLE TRUTH
>
> *An unresolved or uncommunicated feeling will arise over and over again.*

FOR YOUR CONSIDERATION

Because of an unexpressed hurt feeling, you may go out of your way to avoid another person, even when your work depends on that person. Often the matter ends up being a simple misunderstanding.

FIRST STEPS

To transform negative feelings into more positive feelings and behavior, ask yourself:

1. What am I *angry* or *frustrated* about?
2. In what way do I feel *hurt, pain,* or *sadness* about not having or missing something that I want or need?
3. What do I *fear* that is sending a warning to me about possible loss or pain?
4. Might I be feeling *guilt* or *sorrow,* suggesting that I may be responsible for contributing to an undesirable situation?
5. How can I *understand* and *have compassion* for the other person's point of view or feelings?

REFLECTION

To whom at work do you need to communicate your complete feelings about something? Are you holding that person responsible for your feelings? What is holding you back from communicating your feelings to that person?

NEXT STEP

Using the First Steps sequence, draft a statement that transforms a set of unexpressed negative feelings you have about someone at work into more positive feelings.

HUMOR is the ability to *graciously* acknowledge the difficulty or absurdity in a situation without placing the focus or blame on anyone else.

> SIMPLE TRUTH
>
> *The best direction for humor is at yourself.*

FOR YOUR CONSIDERATION

Appropriate humor focuses on building confidence, releasing stress, and enhancing creativity and problem solving.

FIRST STEPS

To maintain a sense of humor when situations get stressful at work:

1. Take a breath.
2. *Don't panic.*
3. Practice responding with the phrase, "That's interesting."
4. Distinguish what is of critical importance and what is of less or no real consequence, and respond appropriately.
5. Try not to take the situation personally; it's usually not worth it.
6. Remember that humor is *not*:
    - Using profanity
    - Teasing or baiting someone
    - Engaging in practical jokes
    - Telling sexist, racial, or ethnic jokes

REFLECTION

What makes you laugh? Why?

NEXT STEP

Describe situations at work that challenge your ability to maintain a sense of humor. Find the underlying humor in these situations.

SENSITIVITY is becoming aware of the *hidden* part of yourself that can sometimes unwittingly affect what you say and how you do things.

> SIMPLE TRUTH
>
> *There are no mistakes, only lessons to be learned.*

FOR YOUR CONSIDERATION

When you break a confidence, spread a rumor, or betray a trust, look for the lesson underlying such behavior.

FIRST STEPS

To become more aware of a hidden side of yourself:

1. Be sensitive to your emotions, especially feelings of lower self-esteem.
2. Become aware of changes in how people respond to you.
3. Consider your own assumptions and expectations of others.
4. Ask for direct and honest feedback about your behavior from someone you respect and trust.
5. Appreciate and honor aspects of yourself that you didn't recognize before.

REFLECTION

Recall a situation at work when your behavior appeared to cause a conflict or problem for someone else. Recall a situation when someone else's behavior seemed to cause a conflict or problem for you.

NEXT STEP

Practice becoming more aware of what underlies your behavior. Acknowledge this awareness to yourself and others.

YOU are the person *ultimately responsible* for your success.

> SIMPLE TRUTH
>
> *The only thing you can know for certain is that nothing is for certain; likewise, it's not what happens to you, it's what you do about it that makes the difference.*

FOR YOUR CONSIDERATION

During a company change, reorganization, restructuring, or downsizing, the people who take a positive, proactive approach often get the best jobs; those who resist get what's left; and those who complain often find themselves without a job. Waiting for a definitive answer as to "what will happen" will decrease your motivation and productivity and make you more vulnerable to being negatively affected by the change.

FIRST STEPS

1. Expect the unexpected.
2. Accept that life is full of ambiguity and contradiction.
3. Pay attention to your thoughts and feelings.
4. Acknowledge and manage your internal critic.
5. Seek to accept and forgive yourself and other people.
6. Continually review and revise your expectations.
7. Learn from feedback and criticism.
8. Explore your needs and wants, and communicate them to others in a clear and honest manner.
9. Appreciate that you are in a constant process of growth and change.
10. Trust yourself to do the right thing.

REFLECTION

Think about a change that might occur at work. What would happen if you took some action in advance? What would happen if you did not take any action? What would not happen if you took action? What would not happen if you did not take action?

NEXT STEP

Describe possible actions you can take to prepare for the unexpected at work.

SESSION SYNTHESIS

- What insights or new awareness did you gain in this session?
- What key learnings are associated with those insights?
- Which Coaching Points or aspects were easier to work through?
- Which Coaching Points or aspects were more difficult to work through?
- What specific steps or actions have you already taken? What occurred or didn't occur?
- What specific steps or actions do you feel most resistant to taking? What is underlying that resistance?
- What questions or concerns remain unanswered for you right now? What are you going to do about it?

COACHING SESSION FOUR

■

Getting Where You Want to Go

In this session you will explore the following Coaching Points:

- ADAPTABILITY
- ROLES
- VOCATION
- LIFESTYLE
- OUTCOMES

The final and most important component of *Being Your Best* concerns the ability to focus on what is important and meaningful to you amid the distractions of what is going on around you. Without a clear focus, you may lose sight of what is in your best interest and find yourself diverted onto a path that leads to a dead end.

The road map for getting to where you want to go takes you through a number of milestones. First, you need to learn how to adapt to changing situations and circumstances. By also understanding and expanding the roles you play at work, you will enhance your ability to become adaptive. As you continue on your personal journey, you will learn to treat what you do as a vocation that has meaning and purpose in your life and that requires you to balance work and lifestyle expectations and trade-offs. By paying attention to all these markers you will keep your desired destination in sight.

ADAPTABILITY is creating opportunities to *transfer* the *talent* and *skill* you already have to other jobs.

> SIMPLE TRUTH
>
> *The more options and alternatives you have, the most flexible and adaptive you can be.*

FOR YOUR CONSIDERATION

Almost every job requires people to have the following skills, knowledge, and attributes: (1) the basic skills of reading, writing, and computation; (2) the interpersonal skills of listening and oral communication; (3) the ability to think creatively and solve problems; (4) comfort in learning computer applications; and (5) demonstration of a "can do" attitude of service.

FIRST STEPS

1. Assess your strengths, qualities, skills, and abilities:
   - What do you like to do?
   - What do you do well?
   - What aren't you doing that you could do?
2. Talk with people who do jobs that interest you:
   - Ask them how they got their job, what they do in the job, and how they learned to do it.
3. Take actions to build on what you already know and can do:
   - Call or meet with someone who can help you.
   - Read an article or a book about your interests.
   - Attend a presentation, meeting, or workshop.

REFLECTION

What are your options for the kind of work you can do and where and for whom you can do it?

NEXT STEP

List the ways you can adapt or build on what you currently know and are able you do.

ROLES are described by the *expectations* you and others have about how and when you perform your work.

> SIMPLE TRUTH
>
> *You may have one job description but many different job roles.*

FOR YOUR CONSIDERATION

Much negative job stress is caused by role conflict and role ambiguity.

FIRST STEPS

To assess any role you may have at work, consider:

1. The *expectations* others have of what you are responsible for and how you should do it.
2. The *interpretation* you have of what you are responsible for.
3. Your *willingness* to perform to those expectations.
4. Your actual *behavior*.

REFLECTION

Consider the various roles you play at work. Which roles seem to fit most closely with your abilities or qualities? What other roles would you like to play that you currently do not? What can you do to change or expand your roles to your advantage?

NEXT STEP

Describe any aspects of your work roles that you need to clarify and state whom they need to be clarified with.

VOCATION is bringing an inner sense of *purpose* and *service* to whatever work or job you do.

SIMPLE TRUTH

Having an inner purpose can guide and support you through difficult times.

FOR YOUR CONSIDERATION

What do you think about the work you do? Is it an occupation, a calling, a trade, a craft, or a profession? Or is it drudgery, toil, a routine, or a grind?

FIRST STEPS

Determine your own sense of purpose in what you do by considering the following:

1. Do you *care* about the work you are doing?
   Why or why not?
2. Are you *committed* to what you are doing? Why or why not?
3. Do you *strive* to do your work well? What inhibits you from achieving your best?
4. Do your *rewards* come from more than just being paid?

REFLECTION

Can you change your attitude toward your work, or should you change your work?

NEXT STEP

Describe what is missing from your job that, if it were there, would offer you a sense of purpose.

LIFESTYLE is a combination of the decisions you make to create *balance* and *health* on a short- and long-term basis.

The challenge is to *evaluate*, at any point in time, the amount of attention and energy you are giving to each of the following aspects of a whole life:

- Work
- Freedom and choice
- Power and influence
- Family, friends and intimacy
- Financial and future goals
- Recreation and exercise
- Health and nutrition
- Social and community service
- Creative and artistic pursuits
- Religious and spiritual practice

SIMPLE TRUTH

Money can't buy you love; love doesn't pay the bills; and without health you can't enjoy any of it.

FOR YOUR CONSIDERATION

Some people are willing to take a pay cut to spend more time with their families. Others work two jobs to maintain a lifestyle or simply survive.

FIRST STEPS

To move toward a work and lifestyle balance:

1. *Prioritize* the aspects listed above in terms of the degree to which they influence your life today: "most," "somewhat," "least," or "not at all."
2. *Evaluate* whether the amount of energy you put into one or another aspect is serving your current needs and wants.
3. *Assess* how well your working relationships *support* your values and lifestyle.
4. Decide to do one or more of the following:
    - *Assert* and negotiate for change to meet your value needs
    - *Accept* work relationships as they are

- *Adjust* your expectations
- *Find* another "reality" somewhere else that better meets your needs

REFLECTION

What are the work-related trade-offs involved in changing aspects of your lifestyle?

NEXT STEP

Describe what you need to change about the work you do in order to bring more balance to your lifestyle.

OUTCOMES are the *specific* results you want to achieve in relation to an objective or goal.

SIMPLE TRUTH

Planning sets your direction.

Taking action gets you there.

FOR YOUR CONSIDERATION

Typical outcomes a manager wants from an employee include (1) doing the right work in the right amount of time; (2) learning new knowledge and skills that can contribute to the company in the future; (3) enjoying the work and interacting well with co-workers; and (4) being committed to doing a good job.

FIRST STEPS

To set and achieve reasonable outcomes:

1. Be very specific in what you want to achieve.
2. Be positive in your attitude.
3. Focus on the desired sensations you expect to feel, see, and hear as you move toward what you want.
4. Collaborate with other people in achieving mutual outcomes.
5. Distinguish between short-term, mid-term, and long-term outcomes.
6. Recognize that long-range outcomes are made up of medium-range outcomes and that medium-range outcomes are made up of a series of short-term outcomes.
7. Review and revise your desired outcomes on an ongoing basis.

REFLECTION

Consider something you are thinking about or hoping will occur at work, but that hasn't happened yet. Examine honestly your feelings and expectations about it.

NEXT STEP

Describe ways that you can make your desired outcome a reality.

SESSION SYNTHESIS

- What insights or new awareness did you gain in this session?
- What key learnings are associated with those insights?
- Which Coaching Points or aspects were easier to work through?
- Which Coaching Points or aspects were more difficult to work through?
- What specific steps or actions have you already taken? What occurred or didn't occur?
- What specific steps or actions do you feel most resistant to taking? What is underlying that resistance?
- What questions or concerns remain unanswered for you right now? What are you going to do about it?

ABOUT THE AUTHOR

MICHAEL BAROFF has 20 years experience collaborating with organizations to achieve business strategy and change management outcomes, work process improvement, and human resource performance results. He applies a unique blend of competencies in the areas of qualitative research, work systems analysis, information synthesis, process intervention and training design, facilitation, dialogue, mediation, and coaching.

He has consulted to numerous companies in a wide range of industries, government agencies, nonprofit organizations, educational institutions, and community groups, including the Internal Revenue Service, Metropolitan Water District, Jet Propulsion Laboratory, Consumer Credit Counseling Service, Prudential Insurance, PacifiCare Health Systems, Nissan Motor Corporation, Federal Express, Xerox Corporation, Blue Cross, Southern California Gas Company, University of California, Armstrong World Industries, Amway, United Way, and the Los Angeles Unified School District.

Baroff is former president of the Los Angeles Chapter of the American Society for Training and Development (ASTD). He has contributed articles on workplace performance improvement topics to the *Society for the Advancement of Management Newsletter*, *Supervisor's Guide to Quality and Excellence*, ASTD *Interchange*, and *The Tao of Dialogue: A Manual of Dialogic Communication*. He has spoken and conducted workshops at conferences and association meetings for ASTD, Center for Nonprofit Management, the State of California Office of Continuous Improvement, the Personnel Testing Council, and the International Society for Performance Improvement. He conducts customized workshops to assist organizations in introducing and integrating the *Inner Work of Work* guidebook material.

The author would appreciate learning about your experiences using this guidebook. Please send your feedback and comments to him via mail, e-mail, or the *Inner Work of Work* Web site.

Michael Baroff
Organization Effectiveness Consulting
2461 Santa Monica Blvd., PMB 337
Santa Monica, CA 90404
(310) 285-8043
Mbaroff@aol.com
http://www.innerworkcoaching.com

THE INNER WORK OF WORK

In *The Inner Work of Work*, experienced organizational consultant Michael Baroff has created a series of three hands-on guides that enables employees to coach themselves on the job, showing them how to develop key competencies in self-management and interpersonal relations, and meet and exceed corporate expectations.

The work employees do "inside"—improving their own attitude, behavior and skills, and understanding of organizational dynamics—pays off in improved performance and greater job satisfaction. *The Inner Work of Work* guides readers in taking over their training and being their own best coaches.

The guidebooks in *The Inner Work of Work* series:

• BEING YOUR BEST helps people become more aware of how their personal attitudes and the choices they make ultimately determine their success. This guidebook enables readers to come to terms with who they are, what they have to offer, and where they want to go in their work lives. They will explore their beliefs about work, what motivates them to succeed, how to use their creativity and intuition, clarify the roles they play at work, learn how to adapt to change, and create the outcomes and lifestyles they want.
Paperback, 64 pages, 6" x 9", ISBN 1-58376-153-5, Item #61535-705, $10.95

• GETTING ALONG WITH OTHERS addresses the behavior and skills that enhance one's communications and relationships with other people. In this guidebook readers examine how their behavior is perceived by others, learn how to develop trust, listen attentively and develop rapport when communicating, set the stage for dealing with differences and conflict, and present themselves assertively when working with others.
Paperback, 64 pages, 6" x 9", ISBN 1-58376-154-3, Item#61543-705, $10.95

• CONTRIBUTING TO YOUR COMPANY'S SUCCESS illuminates the organizational dynamics that create and support a productive work environment. This guidebook enables readers to determine where they fit into a company's big picture, learn how to work as part of a team, understand how a company evaluates the bottom line, determine how to add value in what they do, and develop their own approaches to being a leader.
Paperback, 64 pages, 6" x 9", ISBN 1-58376-155-1, Item #61551-705, $10.95

Order in quantity and save!

10–49: $9.85 (per unit) • 50–99: $9.30 • 100–499: $8.21
500–999: $7.66 • 1000–1999: $7.11 • 2000–2999: $6.57

Call Berrett-Koehler Special Sales for information—415-288-0260.

ORDER THE INNER WORK OF WORK SERIES

Four ways to order:

- **ONLINE** 24 hours a day through our secure server: bkconnection.com
- **CALL TOLL-FREE** 7 A.M. to 12 midnight: 800-929-2929
- **FAX** to 802-864-762
- **MAIL** to Berrett-Koehler Communications, PO Box 565, Williston, VT 05495

EACH GUIDEBOOK IS $10.95

BUY ALL THREE AND SAVE 10% FOR A TOTAL OF $29.50

PLEASE USE THE FOLLOWING IDENTIFICATION NUMBERS WHEN ORDERING:

Being Your Best	ISBN 1-58376-153-5	Item #61535-705
Getting Along With Others	ISBN 1-58376-154-3	Item #61543-705
Contributing to Your Company's Success	ISBN 1-58376-155-1	Item #61551-705
Set of all three	ISBN 1-58376-152-7	Item #61535-705

ORDER IN QUANTITY AND SAVE!

10–49: $9.85 (per unit)	500–999: $7.66
50–99: $9.30	1000–1999: $7.11
100–499: $8.21	2000–2999: $6.57

Call Berrett-Koehler Special Sales for information at 415-288-0260.

BK

Berrett-Koehler Communications, Inc.

450 Sansome Street, Suite 1200, San Francisco, CA 94111

COACHING PROMPTS

As you work through each Coaching Point, you may want to keep this insert at hand so you can refer to the prompts below.

DEFINITION

Coaching Prompt: As you read the Definition, what stands out for you? Note your immediate responses. Do you agree or disagree with this Definition? Does it make you think of any experiences at work?

SIMPLE TRUTH

Coaching Prompt: Does the Simple Truth ring true? If so, describe an experience that makes it real for you. If not, note what situation in your experience suggests something different.

FOR YOUR CONSIDERATION

Coaching Prompt: Think about the practical implications and consequences of the For Your Consideration statement. What experiences, if any, have you had that confirm this statement? Have you had any experiences that suggest this statement isn't always true? Keep in mind that all of the statements within the Coaching Points are only guides; it is your experience that counts.

FIRST STEPS

Coaching Prompt: Read through each of the First Steps and make notes to yourself in response to each question or suggestion.

REFLECTION

Coaching Prompt: Remember that reflection happens best when you are in an open and relaxed state of mind. Sometimes it is hard to make this happen. It can help to take a deep breath and close your eyes for a moment before you begin. Then, read the statement and take some time to look within yourself and consider what meaning it has for you.

NEXT STEP

Coaching Prompt: You should now be ready to outline some Next Steps. Be very specific for each action. Make an agreement with yourself about when, where, and with whom these actions will take place.

Appreciate and acknowledge your progress no matter what pace you move at in your journey. —MICHAEL BAROFF